Management secrets in a turbulent era

Discover the principles of company management as a living organism

LIBOR WITASSEK

Copyright © 2018 Libor Witassek
All rights reserved.
ISBN: 9781986627153

DEDICATION

To key shareholders of
VÍTKOVICE MACHINERY GROUP
without whom this book would have been
completed two years earlier

CONTENTS

1	We know the means, we do not know the goals	1 #
2	Global transformation	7 #
3	The Secret of Planning in a Turbulent Economy	13 #
4	Cognitive strategies	19 #
5	Managerial inertia	27 #
6	Innovations without implementation are hallucinations	34 #
7	Digital Darwin	41 #
8	Organic Change Management Model	46 #
9	Summary and recommendations of the coordinated action	57 #

"Successful business is more the work of biology and evolution, than industrial engineering"

DC VISION

ACKNOWLEDGMENTS

I want to thank all the owners and managers of companies who had the courage to let me into the transformation projects, change management or crisis management in their companies, didn't make it easy for them.

Acknowledgments also include prof. Milan Zelený, who inspired me to change my mind and as a consequence changed my approach to business.

INTRODUCTION

In my more than 25 years of experience in management and in business I have noticed a number of things, trends, management techniques that worked, but also those that did not work. I have begun to observe the ongoing changes, global trends and attitudes, with a certain degree of insight, I was increasingly able to understand the changing environment, understood the principle of cyclical equilibrium, and gradually managed to better predict the future. The economy is a living organism, it is not a machine, so it impossible for a company to be driven as if it were a machine.

Example from practice P.1.

In 2013 I was effective an expert on operational excellence in Turkey, where I implemented changes in a electro technical factory. During my stay, there was the Icelandic volcano eruption that even at a distance of thousands of miles influenced the life in this factory. There was a volcanic ash in the air above Europe, and air traffic was stopped. This company has more than 1,000 suppliers around the world. And so, deliveries gradually cease, resulting in production being stopped within a few days, because the chips did not arrive from Japan and even other parts needed for production. The whole company shuddered and began to spontaneously change, looking for new ways to get back to work, but differently, without the aircraft. The Icelandic volcano eruption caused an incredible positive change – it triggered long-needed changes in the company in Turkey.

And here it started. A last I understood that the **company is looking for a new balance within the vast vibrant global complex network of partners.** In this book I want to share these insights I gathered from my experience and observation. **Everything is about cyclical equilibrium.**

The world evolves very rapidly, but it changes quite logically, and even in seeming chaos, it can be quite predictable. You need to be able to take a good look, understand what is happening in our neighborhood, adapt and take action quickly. I will describe several stories about how the world is changing, about managing in chaos, about knowledge and cognitive strategies.

What this book is not about:

It is not my goal to prove my truth, this book:
- it is not a "how to make the first million"
- does not contain guaranteed "7 habits" types of recipes.
- does not replace well-established common-sense principles.

My endeavor is to share the approaches that have helped me to improve business performance on five continents, even though these processes and tools are not simply transferable because each company is a unique original, created by people and therefore nature.

Still, I will be glad if I succeed to inspire the reader to positive changes without having to wait for another volcano eruption.

1 CHAPTER

We know the means, we do not know the goals

The world has changed

The world's economy is reminiscent of a vast network of interconnected cells, much like the human skin. Deepak Chopra, a world-renowned Indian physician, said in one of his lectures that the skin on human hands would be completely replaced once every two weeks. The skin is made up of millions of cells that are created every day, they connect the human tissue and also vanish. The skin is exposed to relatively aggressive surroundings, frost, rain, heat, sun and wind. The dying of and emergence of new cells is a necessity for a healthy organism. Therefore, every one of us will be in just two weeks in completely new skin, the body constantly maintains its healthy balance. **Balance is key to life, as well as for the survival of the company.**

Similar to the entire economy, with billions of consumers, millions of traders, hundreds of millions of businesses in which billions of people work. Everything works like a huge network of businesses, consumers, suppliers and other players on this global market. And there are other networks: banking, advertising, networking of designers and IT companies, etc. All these networks have been connected through IT technology, thanks to the Internet. **The whole system is huge, complex, cyclically changing, and it is difficult to predict** where the company will be tomorrow, let alone estimate where it will be in 5 years. Many companies make a mistake, many will not understand market developments and will immediately be replaced by another supplier. This practically opens on a daily basis the doors for the competition to enter into the field.

The current external environment in which individual businesses operate is characterized by a **breakthrough dynamics of development: constant change, uncertainty and risk of wrong decisions, increase of permanent competitive conflicts**, etc.

We know the means, we do not know goal

Everything is cyclically changing, managers have problems with prediction of its plans, with prediction of any future. **Continuous linear business environment has changed into turbulent surroundings.**

Classical planning was previously based on extrapolation methods. We have made a turnover of 100 million this year, so we will give you 5% more next year. To estimate future business opportunities time series of cost, cost, innovation development, etc. were used. It was soon realized that the predictions achieved on the basis of these methods are fundamentally impaired by frequent changes in the environment.

Plans are not working out any more, both downwards and downwards, as well as upward when the interest in the new product or business plan is such that it takes months and sometimes years for the company to be able to produce and deliver the product at all. Thus conceived planning, in times of increasing changes in the environment, degenerates into a single purpose. For the "pre-turbulent" time, a linear management model to put emphasis on the procedure, procedure and a well-prepared plan, is fitting, but the discontinuous time fundamentally value of all these processes.

Based on past trends, we cannot reliably predict future developments. An analysis of the past as a tool of strategic management becomes problematic. The target is also uncertain and can only be formulated with greater or lesser probability.

A new type of uncertainty was born: **we know the means, but we do not know the goals.** [9]

Example of practice P.2.

A small Czech manufacturer of aircraft parts for Boeing, Airbus and Bombardier, received orders in 1998 for production for a period of 6 to 12 months ahead. Production planning was fairly easy, it was possible to plan capacities and employees for many months ahead. Gradually the whole supplier chain has changed and 10 years later, the same manufacturer with the same customers receives orders for a maximum of 5 days in advance. Theoretically, over the entire week the orders may not come in and the company will be from day to day without an order. Another complexity of today's time also lies in the significantly greater variability of the manufactured parts. Almost every order is a new original piece, so planning must be done daily and daily it must respond to any deviations.

Global customers require more tailor-made products and services. **Mass customization and individualization** are replacing mass production. First to sell and then to produce (tailor made) is a new paradigm of global competitiveness. [10]

In this uncertain time grows in the importance of organizational and managerial agility and a knowledge worker.

Knowing does not mean to be able

Agility is the ability of a company to change or adapt rapidly in response to market change. Organizational agility is key for businesses and personal agility is becoming a key technology for a successful manager. A high degree of organizational agility helps companies successfully respond to the emergence of new competitors, the development of new changing technology in the industry, or sudden changes in market conditions.

Knowing does not mean to know. Knowledge (ability, skill) is the purposeful coordination of action. The information (cookbook) is just a symbolic description of the event (the ability to cook). There is no difference in nature or in business. [11]

The constantly changing environment is therefore a great opportunity for the emergence of new companies, for the application of new business ideas, own agility and knowledge. Changes in the world economy can be seen as an inspiration for new business, for new opportunities.

Exercise 1 - Turbulent environment

If you are in doubt whether your business is in a continuous or turbulent environment, try answering the following questions:

- Can you plan production with certainty for weeks or months ahead?

- Do you have a small portfolio of products that can be easily planned for production?

- Can you change your production plans by day?

- Do you have small deviations between annual plan and reality?
  (small means deviations in the order of percentages)

- Can you accurately estimate sales with a monthly deviation of less than for example 5%?

If you have answered mostly NO, then your business is likely to be in a turbulent environment. The turbulence indicators are much more, the most important is the ability to accurately predict business results and achieve them with the smallest of deviations. If you cannot estimate the results and the reality is significantly different at the end of the planning period, then there is a high probability that the market is changing so quickly that you cannot adapt in time.

The first recipe for success is to **shorten the planning period** from annual to quarterly, quarterly to monthly or monthly to weekly. It depends on the company and on the environment, how fast it changes.

2 CHAPTER

Global transformation

The first half of the '80s last century, marked an increase in market environment dynamics. PF Drucker (1994) talks about the age of turbulence (discontinuity) and related to **turbulent management.** [3]

The beginning of the turbulence dates back to the late '70s and then with unimpeded intensity, complicates the creation of business competitiveness. The onset is associated with oil and the problems that followed in a total of three waves 1973-74, 1977-78 and the last in 1991 in the context of the Iraq-Kuwait war. These price shocks triggered a significant political, social and economic discontinuity. The consequence of management was the realization that an enterprise could no longer follow the same methods as in the past.

> "Our only certainty is that things will change."
> Philip Kotler

From turbulence to chaos

Continuous changes in the surroundings, an increase in permanent competitive clashes, increase of uncertainty and the risk of incorrect decisions **necessitate the** search for a process of management organization, which would be far better than the current system, responding to the new situation.

Businesses must learn to expect the unexpected. Turbulence, first felt as a threat, becomes a challenge and an ideal business environment for the ready.

Change management has developed a range of techniques and methodologies that are able to meet the above requirements and reiterated prosperity two factors: hard, on the methodology and management techniques and soft, addressing the attitudes and behavior of people. Both planes must be balanced. [9]

Chaos

The second half of the '80s is marked by a further deepening of the turbulence bordering on chaos [6]. In the creation of competition-ability this means that long-term forecasts (the basis of classical planning and strategic management methodology) in this environment are meaningless because it is unrealistic to make a sufficiently probable forecast over a longer period of time with unpredictable developments in the environment. [9]

Order in chaos

The order of chaos and the theory of chaos has become part of modern natural science. It proves that it is from the environment of chaos that the development of society can be organized and a certain order.

This order of chaos is in the unstable conditions a fruitful background for the company's innovative development. Chaos studies have been conducted not only in physics, but also as research into the behavior of vital human organs, the study of economic processes, and many other fields of human activity. **By order, we usually understand such an arrangement of elements and links of the system, in which we can assume knowledge of its further behavior.** So, we can create the right expectations and, with a high probability, expect to meet these expectations. We do not need to know all the elements and links of the system so that we can manage and control its behavior.

When we recognize this system and respect it and in tune with it intercede into the system, it will respond as expected. Order is the result of knowledge, but it does not have the character of law, as in physics, for example.
Chaos refers to a situation where the order does not exist or is unknown to us. **If we do not recognize the order properly or our behavior is reduced inappropriately, we are then not able to predict the behavior of the system or make the right decisions.** [9]

Liquid modernity

Drucker used turbulence metaphor characteristics from the exact sciences to characterize the metaphor. Similarly, Zygmunt Bauman proceeded to formulate the concept of **liquid modernity**. [2]

It is based on the properties of liquids and gases - the so-called fluidity. Fluid properties cannot hold their shape, do not bind space or time, and the flow of time is much more important for the fluid than space. From meeting with solids, the fluids leave undamaged, while the solids change.

Modernity has been a "liquefaction" process from the beginning. The process of "melting bodies" has unleashed a complex network of social relationships. Today there is a redistribution of the "melting forces" of modernity. Everyone has to find his place(niche) in the new order with the help of the newly acquired freedoms [9]. Similarly, the European companies must find their place in an open market world economy.

Z.Bauman's book deals with **five basic concepts of liquid modernity:**

- emancipation,
- individuality,
- time and space,
- work,
- community.

The fluidity (turbulence) of the current relevant business environment is an irrevocable fact and is most likely to deepen in the future.

Autopoiesis

Autopoiesis (from Greek autos-alone and poiin-making, forming) is a term that describes the nature of systems that cannot be explained by external causes, but which are maintained by their own structure. Theories of autopoiesis were formulated by H.Maturana and F.Varela.

System theories distinguish between three types of systems [1]:

- Closed
- Openly
- Autopoietic

Closed systems

They are little differentiated, and interference with the system is also perceived as a threat. Closed system is unable to respond adequately to them. The system is maintained by strengthening the internal order.

Open systems

Relationship with its surrounding is open, the system accepts the environment as a source of new life-giving impulses and stimuli essential to its continued existence and strengthening processes, on which they are running. It is much more internally differentiated than the closed system. The structure is flexible, elastically reacts to environmental changes.

Autopoietic systems

The autopoietic system is highly internally differentiated. does not consider the surrounding as an obstacle to development because it defines and determines itself. It produces problems that it resolves regardless of the environment. It decides for itself what is a problem and what needs to be resolved. [1]

Autopoietic system is a system that creates and it restores itself, for its delimitation are the key links between its elements (not the elements themselves) and its delimitation to the environment. A simple example is a cell, where the exchange of matter between the cell and the cell's surroundings, its ultimate goal is self-preservation and where the links between its elements play a key role. [1]

From a business practice point of view is such a cell an individual or small team. Internal transformations of the system are subject to certain limitations. System located in a certain state may develop only in a certain way. **There are even conditions that the system cannot leave.** These states are called the system states (homeostasis) and represent its equilibrium position. The system may have more of its own states, internal transformations conform to its behavioral norms.

In the case of a **stochastic system** where the resulting state is probable, the system can pass between the individual equilibrium states. The probability of transition between two own states increases with the application of some external impulse. The deeper the steady state of the system, the stronger the impulse must be for the system to deviate from its equilibrium positions and to cause the transition to another state of its own. Intuitively, it is clear that **stochastic systems tend to migrate to the deepest states of their own.** [1]

The key is in corporate culture

Special features have autopoietic systems that are very resistant to impulses coming from outside the system and very unwillingly leave their own states. In such a system the destruction of the system will occur before the internal changes take place. The adaptability of the system is given only by the "width" of its own state. [1]

Example of practice P.3.

A typical business that basically works on 'autopsy' principles is the Japanese Kyocera. Its business system is called in the literature as amoeba system and amoeba management. Amoeba are small teams of 3-60 people who collaborate and run together, based on cellular accounting. Each amoeba has its accounts and statements, and according to these statements decides whether or not it has the right to life. The top management of the company only sets basic rules for behavior and cooperation in the ameba network, the organizational structure is otherwise very flat and low level.

Amoeba that has no results is automatically canceled and reduced, their employees have to find a place in another amoeba where they can add value to their customers. More information about this system is provided below.

The key is in corporate culture

Autopoietic system of the enterprise is organizationally closed, it cannot be changed by the intervention from the outside. They respond negatively to the interventions from the outside, resisting them. On the other hand, autopoietic systems are thermodynamically open. **Replacing an element does not lead to system change.** Within the framework of self-preservation, the basis of the original element is transferred to the new element, or to other elements of the system. Probably everyone has experienced that by changing the problematic employee in a company does not lead to the solution of the problem, nothing happened because the role of trouble maker was playfully taken over by someone else. **The problem is in the corporate culture of the whole system as a whole, not in a single cell.** [1]

The current global transformation of the economy has brought a turbulent environment - fluid modernity, and now it is no longer possible without autopoietics and without autopoietic corporate systems. [10]

Exercise 2 - Global Paradigm
In a number of sectors, markets are changing very quickly, while in some sectors the usual stability and change is relatively small. However, it is necessary to realize that the potential of globalization is exhausted and there is a global transformation that can be observed in some phenomena around us. Try to answer the following few suggestions:

- Customers are demanding more and more products and tailored services, and not before long it will be each and every order - an original
- Customers require interconnection of information systems and full electronic transmission of information between the supplier and the customer
- Customers do not want to buy from intermediaries
- Customers want to manufacture more and more things for themselves
- Our employees must be more and more multifunctional, be skilled in more crafts at once
- Employees require increasingly flexible working hours or work from home
- Customers are demanding shorter delivery times, ideally will order today, will get goods/service tomorrow
- Customers are demanding lower and lower prices

If you observe more of these trends in your company, it is highly probable that your business is in an ever-expanding post-global economy, at the time of global relocation - the return of the economy to the regions.

3 CHAPTER

The Secret of Planning in a Turbulent Economy

The secret of planning in turbulence

Traditional planning was based on historical data. Last year we turned 80, last year, 100, we want to grow, so we'll take the ruler and next year it will be 120?! Hmm, if the clients could hear you. Such smug planning at the time of increasing market changes degenerates to self-purpose. **A company in a storm cannot be driven by a glance at the rearview mirror!**

Thanks to the global transformation we live in turbulent times. Analyzes based on the past are rather useless. Today's world is looking for interconnections and close links between demand and customer, production capabilities and capabilities to respond quickly to everyday fluctuations in demand.

Businesses and production processes cease to be seen as powerful machines and become live organisms - for the first time in world history!

LEAN is no longer enough

Exercise 3 - How to improve quickly in time of turbulence

At the beginning, you need to think and answer the basic questions:

- How well is your company prepared for a new global paradigm?
- You occasionally have difficulty in linking big and ever-increasing turbulence demand and production / operating opportunities?
- Do you also feel that LEAN is bringing less and less financial effects?

Do not you see any more room for improvement? Then look for an external Sensei expert who in intensive 5 days will examine the possibility of improving your business model right in your business. But do not forget that **LEAN** itself **is no longer enough**, linear thinking FINALLY supersedes cyclical thinking.

> "The biggest lesson from building LEAN Enterprise? The view from the outside is absolutely necessary"
> Pilla A. Leitner, Boeing

Impacts of mass customization

Most businesses today try to meet customer needs, meeting mass customization, and make or provide services increasingly more tailored, small-scale or single-item or providing a specific service. It builds its planning systems on the customer's actual requirements, satisfies orders as soon as possible, continuously shortens the running time of orders.
Production is struggling with the problem of changing its plans every week or even every shift. Strongly requires traders to have longer and more reliable sales

forecasts and warrants their production inefficiencies with uncertain business segment forecasts. On Monday, production capacity is overstretched and 3 times more orders than on Tuesday, so it must be produced on Monday even during overtime (and of course it will also pay related bonuses to employees). On Tuesday, however, half of people send home because they do not have enough work for them. This is the waste from which the business department is accused.

The business segment, on the contrary, faces customer complaints for unfulfilled terms or poor quality of "rushed" production. There are fines and penalties, following the promises of unrealistic deadlines for the next contracts, because he wants to keep the customer at all costs in this difficult situation. This wastage is not the fault of the business, but production's.

Planning problem

Top management is puling out their hair at the meeting, as the difference between cause and effect has definitely disappeared.

Everyone is getting bonuses or bonuses, as in the last months and years almost rule.

Where is the problem?

Most businesses today try to meet customer needs, meet mass customization, and make or provide services increasingly tailored, small-scale or single-items or providing a specific service. It builds its scheduling systems on the customer's real requirements, meets orders as soon as possible, continuously shortens the running time of orders.

Classical planning based on extrapolation methods is becoming more and more ironic. Orders on a big series do not come and in those constantly changing conditions lack the ability plan efficiently and produce. Any future and market developments are today difficult to estimate.

To increase performance, it means that long-term forecasts and extrapolation methods, as the basis of classical planning methodology, in the turbulent environment completely lose sense, because creating a sufficiently probable forecast over a longer period of time in the unpredictable development of the environment is simply gazing at the crystal ball.

EXAMPLES lad from practice P.4.

A medium-sized biogas producer has planned a turnover of CZK 240 million next year. In the first months of the year, however, it gained only 50% of planned sales and turnover is therefore very low. What was the reason? Postponing of investments on the part of Polish customers who have decided to wait for EU subsidies. And the situation has been repeated several months in a row, the competent authorities did not issue subsidies, and customers have not confirmed their orders.

The subsidies themselves curb the free market economy, not only because of the delays to the subsidy claimants, but mostly all because of the breakdown of the free market exchange. It leads to unnecessary over-pricing of products and services.

The already turbulent agrarian market has become completely unpredictable, because no one knows when and whether or not subsidies will be given. For entrepreneurs who have become speculators, who do not count on normal market return, but reckon they get 20, 30 or 40% free, but do not know when.

In such an environment it is not really possible to plan effectively. What is a recipe? Focus on markets and products not under the influence of non-market subsidies on those products that really bring high added value to customers.

Business management systems

How to get out of that vicious circle?

The business must be ready to learn to expect the unexpected. Turbulence, initially felt as a threat, becomes a challenge and an ideal business environment for prepared managers and entrepreneurs. Managing this situation is becoming a key competitive advantage.

Do not know what will happen in a month? Excellent, this is a great opportunity!

The current state of the business environment (turbulence, chaos, fluid modernity) leads to a fundamental change in the management philosophy of organizations. Even in chaos, effective order and order can be built. This order is the basic innovation cornerstone for further development of the company. However, it is not enough to stratify (process) processes using statistical methods of Six Sigma, nor is the LEAN tool nowhere near enough. [5]

By order, we usually understand the arrangement of the elements and links of the system in which we can assume knowledge of his next move. Enterprise is not a machine with simple input - process - output. Even in a complex system of elements and links we can create the right expectations and with a high probability to assume that we will meet these expectations. We do not need to know all the elements and links of the system, so we can direct and control its behavior. When we recognize and respect this system, and work in harmony, it will respond as expected. Such an order may be an efficient **corporate governance system**. [9]

Causes and consequences

Chaos refers to a situation where "order" does not exist, or we simply do not know it. If "order" is not properly recognized or our behavior is disproportionate, we are not able to predict behavior or make a correct decision about it.

Often mistaken decision making is the result of misunderstanding of the links in the whole system, mistaken substitution of causes and consequences, lack of logical thinking. Chaos can be an enterprise where we do not know the links between the different parts of the system, or between the causes and consequences that simply lack a functional business management system.

What is the difference between cause and effect?

The causes and consequences are a series of events that follow. The cause is anything that will trigger a subsequent event. The result is the result of this event. Our whole life is a series of causes and consequences same as the life of the business. If we want to change the result, we must first change or eliminate the causes, not the consequences.

One of the tools for searching for the root cause is the 5x Why [5] method.

Exercise 4 - 5 x Why

Finding the cause of the problem is a basic step for its solution. Tool 5 x Why is it primarily to think about the problem. Insist on adhering to this tool for any problem you will be discussing.

A typical procedure is as follows:

- Define the problem: "We did not complete the task within the required deadline"

Questions 5 times why:

- Why did not we meet the deadline? Because the material came too late for production
- Why did the material come late? Because the purchase was made late
- Why was the purchase ordered late? Because he did not have the financial department approval
- Why did he not have the approval of the financial department? Because we waited for the decision of the manager who was on the business trip

- Why was it not approved by someone else? Because we do not have a defined substitutability ...

As you can see, in this company there are more problems to solve than it seemed at first glance. Failure to meet deadlines is a typical illness of poorly managed companies, and it is often necessary to change many processes and, above all, the causes before removing the visible effect.

Changing the management philosophy

Chaos refers to a situation where "order" does not exist, or we simply do not know it. If "order" is not properly recognized or our behavior is disproportionate, we are not able to predict the behavior of the system or make proper decision about it. [9]

In a rapidly changing environment, the existing approach to managing has to be substantially altered and replaced by a new one. **The traditional organizational hierarchical pyramid, in which commands go from top to bottom, is no longer enough.** You need to try new principles, integrate process management, LEAN & Six Sigma principles, support the work of autonomous teams, the internal market, master infrastructure, including Big Data and IT technology and a number of other steps.

The rate of change in the market (cause) results in more pressure to introduce self-management principles into corporate teams (consequence). Without effective control, however, there is chaos, **self-management is not that everyone is doing what they want**. It is therefore important to maintain control over autonomous teams, balancing their creativity and their performance in real time.

Behavior in a changing environment can not only be predicted but also effectively managed!

4 CHAPTER

Cognitive strategies

Value added

In 1992 Stan Shih (CEO of ACER) published this image with a definition of added value and activities that bring higher and lower added value.

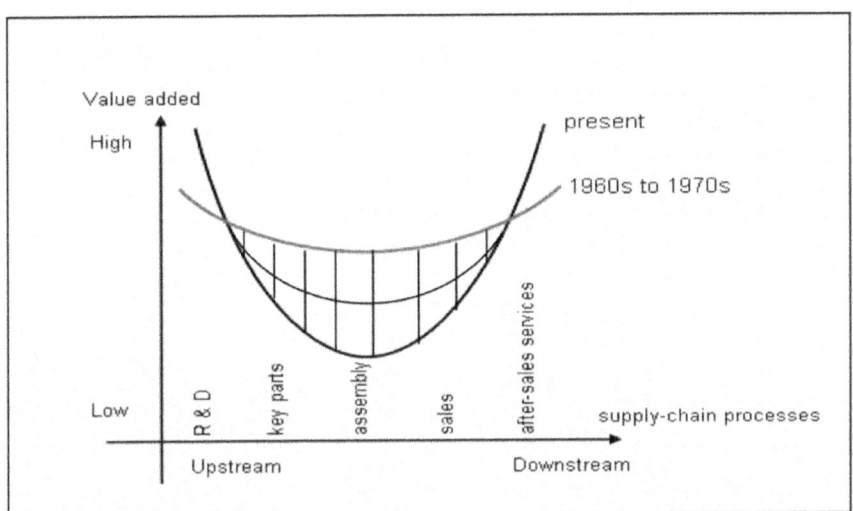

"Manufacturing" has been outsourced to the cheap labour countries by global businesses, and a significant part of the industry in these countries is not, as a matter of fact, an enterprise of its own but only manufactories, with robots or without robots, i.e. **low-value assembly shops.** Only R & D investments can be made from this position.

The word "manufactories" does not include companies that lack automation or other advanced technologies, but companies that provide this kind of service are called "outsourcing" with a low share of their own research and development for global and multinational companies. **In the case of turbulence, manufactories are the first to be turned off by the global corporations, ie turn off the at the switch.**

If an enterprise does not have its own product or service, it does not have a brand and has no access to the customer, then it is by definition **"manufactory"**, although they are sometimes equipped with state-of-the-art manufacturing technologies.

Markets are changing every moment

Example of practice P.5 .

In the past I visited several European manufactories, their stories are often similar. One of them - the manufacturer of leather car seats - has recently laid-off over 2,000 employees, with only 200 workers left and waiting for further instructions from its headquarters in Asia.

A short while ago, the managers in this manufactory have been preparing a new strategy for the year 2018, which expected growth of 15% in 2018, as well as growth in earnings and employment. They have been working on this strategy for more than 2 months, but in just a few days everything changed. The global client has disconnected the manufactory's power supply from the socket as quickly and as easily, as it can disconnect the power cable from the computer.

Why does PowerPoint not have a new strategy?

Not only in manufactories, but in many European companies, **managers lack the skills of cognitive strategies.**

"We live in an objective world that we can recognize and where we can take cognitive steps, in a

world, that works independently from us, observers." Humbero Maturana

Managerial inertia

Current world markets are highly turbulent, demand varies from day to day, often from hour to hour. Successful business today is the one that can respond most quickly to market anticipations and signals in a totally discontinuous environment. Loss of organizational agility means gradual dulling of senses, inability to respond to market signals, and inability to act quickly, means a company ending in a state of market and **managerial inertia of " inertia "**.

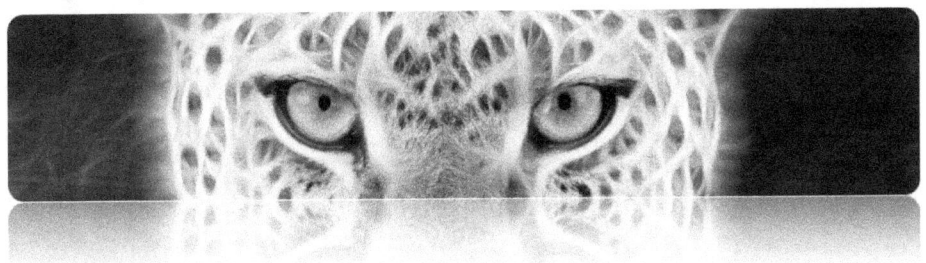

Today's markets are often unpredictable, just as the situation in the wild African savannah is changing.

Cheetahs are in this harsh terrain successful despite the fact that they have no strategy drawn up on 30 slides in MS PowerPoint, have key performance indicators and (KPI) showing that in 2017 cheetah family catches 185 impala, zebras 68 or 19 antelope. The Cheetah family also did not build a team profile according to Belbin, nor does it have a trained typology according to MBTI, yet - or rather because of it - successfully attacks!

Cognitive strategies

How to do it?

Evolutionally successful predator cannot think mechanically and begin to sort his behavior into 16 boxes from the questionnaire or 9 frames in the team profile. Before they make it, even the impalas are long gone.

On the contrary, he thinks and acts organically and concentrates all his efforts-as well **as a competent manager** -especially on detailed **market observation, targeted adaptation, and the use of every opportunity which he cannot afford to waste!**

If a cheetah family, like a number of European companies, got into a state of inertia , it would soon die. There is no difference in nature or in business. The state of " inertia " is the result of managerial behavior, not the cause.

What is missing? Cognitive strategies such as the ability of targeted action.

Any company and management anywhere in the world can get into the state of inertia. To achieve change, focus on cognitive strategies, purposeful and coordinated actions in collaboration with your clients, anywhere on our planet, full of amazing opportunities. Changes are permanent and necessary both at the organization level and at the individual level.

A range of managing methods allows us to name " what we are, " but does not answer the question " how can we change? " Managerial typology answers the question " who we are " but does not provide useful information " how to make our communication skills more effective ". Good typology does not give managers "stickers" of a particular style or type. On the contrary, it offers the possibility to use individual communication styles for effective observation, quick adaptation and effective targeted action.

Modulation/ Variation strategy

Let's go back to the cheetah, which was mentioned in the previous chapter. On TV Prima I watched the documentary about the predators. On the African savannah, the mother of two small cheetahs, slowly approaching the antelope that grazed in the open countryside. The antelope could see all three cheetahs very well, and the predators did not try to hide. The crouching slim bodies of the predators with their eyes fixed on the nearby but difficult prey. Relatively long observation was followed by body straightening and a sharp lunge in which the cheetah reaches a speed of up to 110 km / h for a maximum of 20 seconds. **It's the fastest terrestrial animal in the world!**

What is the real strategy of this predator? **It is a differentiation strategy**, the art of adaptation to the tough conditions, and the ultimate unique ability to achieve a significantly higher speed in 20 seconds. Ability to win in the most sophisticated system our planet has ever created.

Example of practice P.6.

In this I recall the company of my friend, who has complained for many years that the prices of the products have fallen again and there is no longer any room for profit margin. In all, the effort of "perfect" LEAN somehow isn't enough. Huge global supply chains have spread across the planet, demand for individual products and services is only "take it or leave it". Does he have a bad strategy? No, it's just manufactory.

Strategy is what you do

Not just on the example of predators, it is clear that **strategy is what we do** and because we all do something, then we all have a strategy too. Is it enough to just have a good strategy? It's not enough! Today it is not enough to do the right things and do it right. There is a need to look for uniqueness, art to be the best in the world. **Relying on existing and running processes is a hazard with the future of a company!** [11]

So it was enough to ask my friend just one question, "In what is your company the best in the world?" The answer did not come, on the contrary, I learned that customers are choosing the same products and services from a number of other companies. Then there is nothing more than to constantly fight over the price, reduce costs and sit with stress waiting to see what the prices will be on the market tomorrow, what will arrive in the email from the foreign headquarters ...

Do you have similar feelings like my acquaintance? If so, then just consider the 4 basic steps to strategically differentiate:

- **Who am I?** Information isn't enough, coordinated action has to follow. Then build a map of key activities according to Michael Porter,
- **What is my standing?** Now comes the comparison with the competition but where to take the data? Try benchmarking,
- **What is my performance?** Comparing key indicators with competitors gives an answer, what is the situation on the market, who are the best and who the worst players in the market,
- **How can I distinguish myself?** Strategic diversification using radar charts and graphs will determine the strategy.

Forget the new PowerPoint, that's just a description of the action, but you'll have to start a real action!

What is knowledge

Knowledge is coordinated action!

Economies and businesses are living organisms, they are extensive cognitive (self-learning) systems, and as living organisms they must be perceived and controlled. How does cognitive behavior occur in nature?

The document on the Siberian Amur Tigers can be read about cognitive behavior. The Siberian tiger weighs up to 360 kg, with a length of up to 4 meters, making it up to 2 times larger than the so-called "king" of the animals the lion. The Siberian tiger's diet includes bears and black bears, much larger animals than the tiger himself, in his teeth he can carry up to 3 times heavier animal than he is. Evolution has assured the tiger's survival by giving them important skills. With strategic differentiation - it is the largest feline in the world and the added **knowledge to survive** in extremely harsh and unforgiving Siberian nature that made them indisputable and real "King of the Taiga".

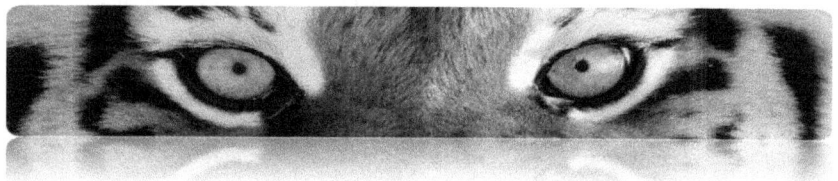

Do you think the Tiger made a business plan for 2014, set performance indicators for KPI, presented dozens of slides in MS PowerPoint to catch 16 bears, 256 salmon and 439 hares?

Information is not an action

I think the tiger is concentrating all his efforts - like a capable manager - on **detailed market observation, targeted adaptation**, and the **use of each opportunity provided. He cannot afford to waste!**

All strategies are often just descriptions of actions, not action itself. Knowledge (ability, skill, um) is a purposeful coordinated action. Information is just a symbolic description of the action. There is no difference in nature or in business.

Knowing does not mean you able to!

In 2013, I was approached by a large manufacturer of rail transporter to help managers and owners create a new strategy. We started a series of workshops where I tried to find leaders in the team who wanted to make decisions and take action. Even after a few days, have failed to find such leaders. Although everyone knew what they wanted to produce, I understood that this is a self-propelled corporate culture that cannot be changed by an outside intervention, the destruction of the system must take place by changing the company on the inside.

Strategy is what you do, not what you write in PowerPoint. [11] And **what you do is what you believe**. Customers do not buy what you produce, but what you believe.

Once you think about your new strategy, think about **what you believe, ask yourself, " Why? "** It is only then that you need to think about the **added value for the customer, i.e. the question " How? "** Well, and finally it's quite easy to answer **" What will we make? "**

Apparently, nothing complicated, but it need the leaders to have the courage to make decisions.

Exercise 5 - Answer to the question " Why? "

There are different ways to succeed in business. Try to reflect on the questions below. One way is to find a market niche, a market place where there is no one is yet.

- Do I have a product that no one else has thought of?

Nowadays, the answer to this question is very often negative. In the global world, it is increasingly difficult to find a product or service that no one in the world knows.

Another option is a road called the "Blue Ocean Strategy". It is the use of benchmarking (comparison with competition), where the characteristics of the product or service are chosen and their comparison with the competitive characteristics is made. You can then decide to excel in some of the features or create an unrepeatable combination of features and offer them on the market.

- What characterizes my product or service?
- Why do customers buy or should buy?
- How can I evaluate the characteristics of my product or service compared to competitors?
- How do I create a unique combination of these characteristics?

An example of a strategic benchmarking chart for online products:

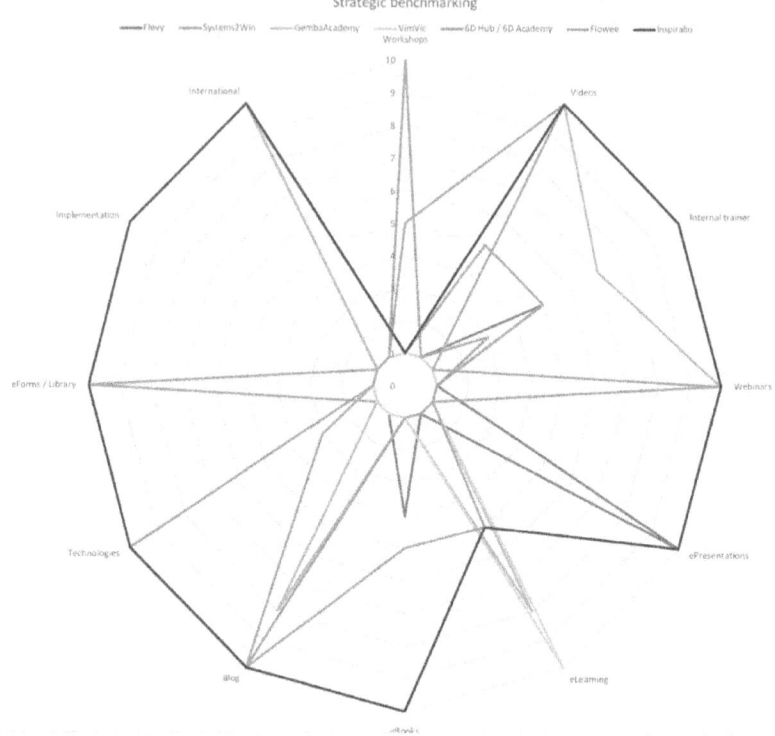

The third way is to find the attributes in a business that were used to be tens of years ago and will be valid for decades and to invest in these attributes, making them the best of all. An example of Amazon, invests in speed, reliability and convenience. And it is the best in the world.

- Which attributes in my business are unalterable and are valid?

5 CHAPTER

Managerial inertia

When the managers do nothing

Organizational inertia is a trend where an advanced organization slides along its current and long-lasting trajectory of inertia. The cause is managerial inertia. Sometimes this **managerial inertia** leads to a situation where the development of the company stops completely or is very static and then it is just a step away into the spiral of death.

It's like steering a car with a cruise on 80 km / hr, but the driver did not notice that he was no longer traveling along the county road but had been driving for a long time on the highway. Such a driver tends to crash on a flat section rather than on a winding and uneven road, even though it runs at a constant and relatively slow speed.

This often leads to managerial inertia just in times of economic growth, when a company moves, goes quietly "on a straight road". Surely you can believe it will be even better. But faith is not an argument.

Economic growth brings with it the ubiquitous deception that the environment does not change or the deception that our economy is changing slowly.

Try to increase your productivity by another 30%!

The opposite is true. **The current transformation from globalization to the relocation of economic activities has taken on a rocket pace**, as we can see in all advanced economies, but today in China as well. Mass customization, digitization, additive manufacturing technologies, the Internet of Things, automation of knowledge work, and dozens of other advanced technologies completely change the economy, at an ever-higher speed. **There is only a lasting innovation, constantly changing processes, services and products.**

Managerial Signals of Inertia

Exercise 6 - Managerial Infertility Signals

What are the signals of managerial inertia?

Beware of the warning signals you see in the company! If you hear some of these passwords, please note:

- Do not fix that, what works!
- It is not possible! We have tried it a few times!
- I know the manager is weak, but I do not have a better one!
- It's been with us for a long time, we have to let it go through the decision-making process.
- We do not have much to do with the timetables
- Six Sigma projects do not bring financial benefits
- Numbers of Kaizen grow, but financial benefits are declining
- We know why, we just do not know what and how
- I do not risk and so I do not make mistakes
- and amazingly "We **are the biggest and best on the market!** " ☐

If you answer YES multiple times, then it's time not only to become alert, but before anything you need to make rapid radical changes. In your company, it is likely to become inert to stimuli both inside and outside.

Eliminate inertia

How come out of it?

Several tips for overcoming the "inertia" status:

- Forget the parent company's history and resources. **For new innovative ideas and projects, start a brand-new business with new people!**
- If the company leader is satisfied with the status quo, it will transfer it to the entire organization, so **be permanently dissatisfied!**

- Many executives in multinational and large corporations have not the courage to change anything fundamentally, waiting for the "top" command. **Look for people who have the craving and courage to break down the implemented, people with spunk.**
- **Kill bureaucracy**, look for new approaches for quick innovation!
- If you see that the manager is not moving, introduce **"job rotation"** or finally fire him! ☻
- Differentiation of the cause from the consequence is the basis of logical thinking, and a change of behavior is necessary in order to survive. Some skepticism is always in place, but it should not obscure the logic of thinking. If you do not change anything, the state of inertia will soon come, or will never die. It should not be difficult to understand.

Faith (and LEAN) is no longer enough, it is necessary to shut down the cruise control finally and step down on the gas ☐

Example of Practice P.7.

Managerial inertia cannot be eliminated simply by relying on the fact that employees are aware of the difficulty of the situation or the bad situation in the company. On the contrary, such an environment of skepticism and survival without a vision is just a breeding ground for the growth of managerial inertia.

The business director of one of the largest engineering firms told me in the pre-insolvency situation of the company during the process audit: " Mr. colleague, why change something, we have experienced this crisis many times. Finally, it will help us to save the company. " Relying on state assistance is the survival of the socialist centrally planned economy, and it is a pattern of thinking that survives today in some companies.

The state did not save anyone, and the company soon ended in bankruptcy. They are billions of crowns; unfinished power plants have turned into concrete monuments in Europe. With hundreds of employees out of work and the company, which survived a whopping more than 100 year, suddenly disappeared.

Changing people's thinking is the most difficult task of today's world leaders. This is not just about socialism, it is about understanding the cyclical movement of the global economy, its overall transformation from globalization to local production using powerful technologies.

In a market economy there is no obligation to survive!

Measurement matters

Why are not plans fulfilled? Because managers are lying

How many times have you seen a situation where you saw a manager lying about the real state of affairs or the gravity of the situation?

Very often you have heard the assurance that the situation is not so hot, and everything will be resolved, you do not need to worry about anything. I'm sure you have experienced many of these situations. As a result of the inactivity of these "guaranteed" reports, there are often criminal offences, damaged reputation with customers or astronomical economic losses.

Managers have a choice between being a respected and honest leader or being popular.

The manager, who has good relationships and is generally popular, sometimes has difficulty to be honest. Whatever the choice, sooner or later there is an undeniable reality. **Eventually the market decides, the truth is in the customer, no matter how cruel.**

"History is a series of agreed lies"
Napoleon Bonaparte

What you do not do, you do not manage

Measure, manage, check!

When evaluating your job, the manager can spread optimistic moods and rumors for a fair amount of time, but in the **Management by Objectives** system, reality will eventually show in full light.

Then comes the other usual " why me? " Reaction, " nothing to do, it's not my fault!" . In other words, in the eyes of that manager, the truth in the form of undisputable reality has nothing to do with the evaluation of his work. **For everything, a company** that " forces" managers to lie, poorly set processes, a bad atmosphere or inefficient corporate culture **can do everything**. **Even spice up the accusation of the customer** " I have done everything as good as possible, the customer does not understand!". All negative reviews are a total lie, the company even forces other employees to lie, and eventual expulsions are totally unfair.

A good manager is aware of the basic fact that managers are often carriers of bad news. If the manager only has good news, One should automatically be suspicious. Managers have general tendencies to exaggerate the job of others, create purposefully internal competition and tension, often distort distorted information not only towards higher management but also to employees or customers. **Over time they manage to create an atmosphere in the company that it is no longer easy to tell the difference between truth and lies.** That was their goal, to create chaos and confusion, in which only they know, and any evaluation can be without any difficulty doubted.

Culture of accusation

What are the most common manager lies?

An absolute majority of people think they are better than others. That's absolutely natural. Even in the Management by Objectives environment, we cannot avoid any lies. We can rely on our own managerial intuition, but also be alert when we note some of the following signals:

- **I decide on facts, I'm rational!**

Determining the facts is certainly a very necessary and rational strategy. In fact, however, a number of managers are deciding on facts that are readily available, not those that are difficult to access but are important and have a causal link with the desired goal.

- **We are better than our competitors**

Every company is a living organism. It is not easy to judge who is better, not at all by a few metrics such as turnover or profit. The living organism is not static, our information about the state of competition is at least 1 day old, today is not yesterday that was long ago.

- **This is not my fault!**

When things get better, we are happy and proud of our results. We are convinced that we have worked hard and deserve special rewards if they do not come, then we are angry. On the other hand, if they fail, they may always have special circumstances, the market, the customer, or someone else. We are convinced that we should not be penalized in any way. This is a relatively widespread basic attribution error known in psychology for decades. It is useless to be surprised.

Waste of talent

And another lie, the most beautiful:

- **I do not make any mistakes!**

It is really possible that you have a manager in the team who did not make any mistakes. But then he does not take risks. Even a small child learns to walk and so it falls occasionally. The first thing to learn is that a toddler, "how do you safely flop down on ass." Those who do not risk not only do not make mistakes, but they cannot "safely flop down on their ass" . And one day, a crash will happen on, in which the "nose will get bloody" and it will be very dangerous, not just to the flawless manager, but probably to the whole company.

How get out of it?

A good leader has only two ways to reduce the number of lies in the business that are primarily distributed by low-performance managers. The first option is to **direct directives or mentor** these managers in the right direction. **Forget about the nice words, forget about this unnecessary coaching in this case. It takes real action.** To give them just one last chance, they either immediately stop lying, grabbing the reality, and some time they will meet their KPIs, or then it's only the second chance. **In another company, these managers will do much better, you are wasting their current potential and talent, allow them to grow elsewhere simply by firing them!**

No third path exists, so if you want to increase your business's performance. If you do not want to, then the company is also wasting your potential.

Why is it so long for some managers to prepare their goals (KPIs) why is the cascading of goals in so many companies so extremely difficult and lengthy? I think the answer is obvious.

Exercise 7 - Set up KPIs

Key performance indicators are, above all, "key", so they cannot be too many. Ideal for one business process is to set 3-5 KPIs to be followed:

- **How to set KPIs for the production process**?

It's easier than it seems at first glance. The production process has been for centuries productive, quality, continuous time of orders, costs and other parameters. Nowadays, work safety and health protection are often a key set of performance indicators.

That is why you will always start with these basic KPIs and set an assessment interval of these indicators (daily, weekly, monthly). Always compare plan versus reality.

- **How to set KPIs for services and administrative processes?**

The customer comes first. So which process performance parameters are important to the customer? We can also define quality, customer satisfaction, claim (quality), cost or speed of service.

Create a team with which to define these attributes of the non-production process, and set a measurement interval, set a plan, and measure reality.

Everything should be visual! KPIs are better to visualize graphically.

6 CHAPTER

Innovations without implementation are hallucinations

Speed of innovation is growing

The key management issue of today is the speed of innovation. For example, in the 80s of the twentieth century has been shortened product life cycle in general engineering by 32.4% in 10 years, it is now the same pace accelerating spiral of innovation in this sector in just two years.

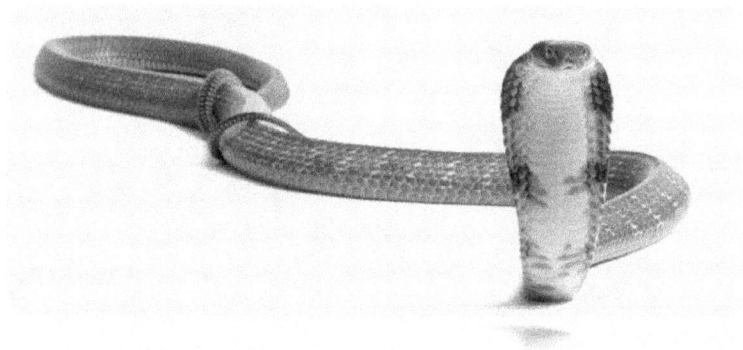

The most powerful and most agile systems have created - as always - by the nature. The feared Indian cobra, feeding on small rodents, will develop the speed of its deadly attack of up to 50 km / h, the usual permitted speed of a car in the village.
Speed is, however, also the weapon that can load a small animal to catch the cobra. Such a smart animal is mongoose, the mongoose is a social creature, wandering in family groups of up to 30 animals. Still, she often finds herself a

cobra and her cobra run, and eventually kills her as her own food. A single mistake and bite of the Cobra would be the exact opposite.

LEAN is not sufficient anymore

In what is the success of the small predator? The speed and the ability to perceive stimuli in context of an interconnected network 30 mates on the same battlefield - as successful business market cooperating in the supply chain.

Global Supply Chain (SCM) is changing rapidly, the rate of change exponentially increases. Why? Because the center of change is a modern consumer. He does not only buy the final product, but thanks to mass customization, he decides on any article in the global Supply Chain.

Small business managers wake up in the morning, they decide to buy new machines, and for a couple of weeks the new machines are spinning. And though the captains of large corporations in the " market uncertainty " often have no choice but to try, at least in the great storm water drain.

Whether you are a cob or mango, you need to match your product innovation lifecycle with your product lifecycle on your market.

> "The big ones do not eat the small ones, it's the faster ones that eat the slow ones!"
> Bill Gates

Innovators of the future

Just learn from history. About 150 years ago, the main means of transport was a horse carriage.

It was not very comfortable and so the manufacturers upgraded it gradually. Likewise, they were cultivating "stronger" horses. And then came a "major" innovation in the form of horse carriages, which today is defined by Wikipedia as a comfortable, suspended four-wheeled passenger car (non-motorized vehicle) driven by horses. Where is their end today? Investors and business are long gone.

Autonomous transport and electromobility

On the way to new markets there may also be intermediate levels. Europe is now developing gas cars, formerly LPG, today a much more dynamic CNG supported by government interventions. Here is room for the really agile and fast companies. Market is rapidly saturating and its development is already influenced by the onset of significantly higher-cost electric vehicles with a significantly lower range, but with a significantly higher potential for investment appreciation.

The investment of "big boys" is now taking place in new batteries (Giga-factory in Nevada) and in all possible electric vehicles (Tesla, Nissan, and many others). **However, innovators of the future are already working on hydrogen articles.** The oil lobbies are struggling with ever lower demand for oil, prices are falling, with this sector linked infrastructure investments being halted or postponed indefinitely.

The emergence of new disruptive technologies can no longer be stopped.

Hidden Crisis Signals

Exercise 8 - How Do You Identify Market Transformation?

He who does nothing, he will not ruin anything, but he does learn nothing. And the market is the best teacher, it is enough to **follow** with humility and respect. The most common market transformation indicators for the selected product are:

- The substitution product is dynamically growing on the market, although it is significantly more expensive,
- Innovation of products or services no longer brings higher margins or sales,
- the customer circle is still the same or decreasing,
- long-term margins and total market size is dropping,
- Development departments (R & D) are more likely to solve the argument why not to do something rather that the opposite,
- Technicians bring dozens of design change ideas that did not originate primarily from customers,
- stock turnover is declining; old unprofitable stocks are growing, which are depreciated in the form of "tiny rain"
- The sales price is already so low that neither outsourcing to Asia nor hundreds of Kaizen will able to move it,
- The speed rate of Innovation is already very low, but customers leave the innovative model series, and such like.

If the manager records 2, 3, or more of these early warning signals, you need to act quickly.

Innovation with action

Nothing new, but those innovations that will not increase competitiveness-ability, do not add value nor increase productivity <u>are not</u> innovation. In addition, **innovations without implementation are not innovation.**

Many executives complain that they have been constantly improving productivity and quality over the last 20 years. Each year they add 3-7% in productivity, in quality, a number of sectors they have shifted only over the past 5 years far below the previously impregnable Six Sigma. Will it never end?

It will not end. Advanced technologies, but above all a change in managerial behavior, are the only way to change the current routine and processes that are not enough in the current world to get in the first league. Productivity growth of another 30% is not only possible, but even necessary, as well as other changes.

However, the problem of frozen productivity or quality is a removed problem, not a causal one. Action is missing.

"Innovation without implementation is hallucination"
Libor Witassek

Cognitive behavior

How to do it?

The foundation is cognitive strategy. The ability to monitor customer behavior and respond immediately, in real time.
The ability to respond instantly leads most of today's managers to a full commitment to process of innovations, primarily to shorten lead time, time from order to delivery date to the customer. Lead time is the time from the start of the process to its complete termination, i.e. the delivery of the goods to the customer, or the complete provision of the service. In order to do this, the company's internal resources are not enough, it is necessary to reduce inventories, or to change the whole chain of supply chain behavior.

How is it related to cognitive strategies? Simply, the **ability to notice change in customer behavior, to understand it immediately and to adapt quickly is just** that **cognitive strategy** [11]. It is in vain to wait for the situation to calm down again and the next time will have more time.

"Strategy is what you do"
Milan Zelený

Faster, cheaper, better

Time is money!

Example of practice P.8.

Yes, in China, they can produce more cheaply. But how long and how much does it cost transport to Europe or to established markets? Ship transport lasts for months, and this is a possible success for European manufacturers. Produce quickly and reliably. This benefit is now being enjoyed by many manufacturers of plastic windows, or even computers. Mammoth computer makers in Europe are able to deliver cloud servers within 1-2 days from the order.

Faster, cheaper, better! The magic formula of today's business world. Goals that no one is discussing are still so difficult to reach. If we want to improve the quality, we cannot be faster. If we want to be cheaper, we cannot want a higher quality. If we want to do better, we cannot be cheaper. We just **have the feeling that we are hitting some "but"** why it is not possible to combine this " holy trio ".

Why?

Planning in the current environment of highly turbulent demand is the speculation from a crystal ball. Reports with historical data, even more and more sophisticated, lead to erroneous planning, unbalanced production and chaos in company's processes. Interpolation of past to future data ceases to work, variations vary every day, every hour.

> **Lead Time is a helper, not a goal. Shortening Lead Time is not a magical wand that will completely change your world.**

Lead time is not enough

For what is the short lead time, though it not required by the customer who wants "his" quality? **There is still a need for customer interest, quality is just and only his property.** Traders say they sell twice as much if we cut delivery times by half? Really? I wish it was that simple.

Short lead time? OR QUALITY? OR low price? OR A WONDERFUL PRODUCT? Perhaps once it was enough. Today the situation is different.

Today's customers want low lead time AND ~~OR~~ **low price AND** ~~OR~~ **best quality AND** ~~OR A WONDERFUL PRODUCT OR SERVICE~~ . That this can´t be done at the same time? It has to work, the words "does not work" are the past.

> "Begin by imposing a fine for every "it does not work" of 20 € "
> Libor Witassek

Better to decide badly than never

Lovers of horses know the opinions of some horse owners, " I'd rather do nothing with the horse than to do something wrong and maybe ruin the horse." It is perfectly understandable, the **most popular activity of a number of people in management is "do nothing".**

What is the basis for success?

- **Customer focus** - There are dozens of ways to track our customer's behavior, from social networks to physical contact with them. Customer

  behavior monitoring, and immediate responsiveness are much more than just lead time. Concentrate on your customer, not your boss.

- **Teamwork** - Every co-worker must understand that he is also a co-entrepreneur. Change your employee into entrepreneurs.

- **Liability** - In a complex organizational structure, at many levels of the organization, the basic behavior is shifting responsibility to others. End the culture of "I cannot do that" into the "I Want It" Culture.

- **Openness towards change.** Nobody likes change, let alone welcome it with enthusiasm. But without change it simply cannot continue. Afford the opportunity to the people who are eagerly seeking out the changes and who are ready for them.
- **Discipline**. Without functional processes it does not work, you do not need heroes who do incredible things. **Sort out your processes properly and you do not look for heroes.**

7 CHAPTER

Digital Darwin

Managers of Harvard Management School support primarily management based on "objectively verifiable data".

The job of a manager and the leader has a different point of view. We work with people, observe them, talk to them, teach managers, and we learn ourselves. What I've noticed:

- **More and more sectors around the world are in a period of strong market turmoil.** Predicting plans are becoming increasingly difficult, especially as part of a globally interconnected society,
- More and more managers are under brutal pressure from customers, on price, on timeliness, on the quality and accuracy of delivery of customer orders,
- More and more managers do not understand their customers, cannot read their behavior, habits and needs, they cannot adapt to changes in modern society.

"The survival does not depend on the strongest of species, nor the most intelligent but the adaptable to change. "
Charles Darwin

Return on Investment (ROI)

Is it still about numbers, return on investment (ROI) or simple survival?

The emergence of new technologies is not about the future, it is the presence. We are witnessing the fascinating transformation of the entire global economy, which is driven forward by new digital technologies. An absolutely crucial aspect is the merging of the physical and virtual worlds into the new virtual world of **cyber-physical systems.**

The following figure shows only a few changes that are now common not only in production:

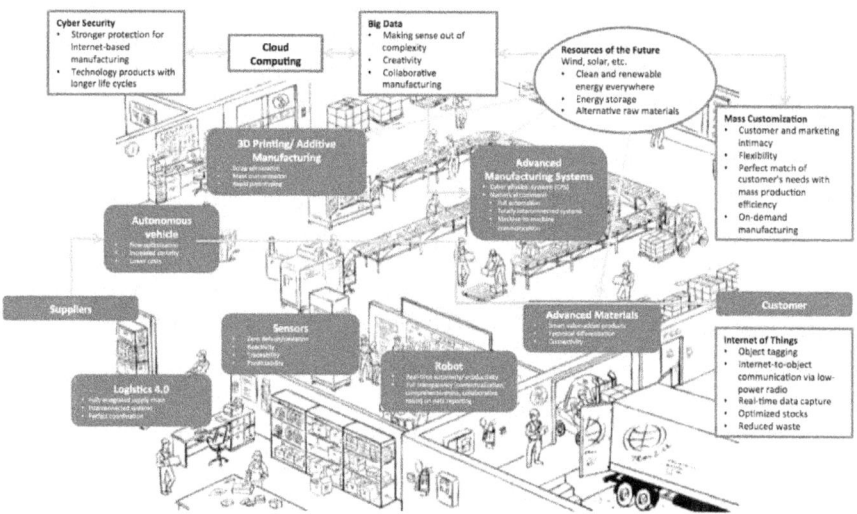

Decentralization

These trends have "disturbing" impacts on every part not only of manufacturing companies. **In just three years of Industry 4.0's first mention, we have seen dozens of new technologies that bring productivity gains of up to 30%,** dramatically higher added value for customers, new experiences and experiences for consumers.

Use of a fusion of the physical and virtual world requires knowledge of new technologies, not only known **3D printers**, but also **technology M2M** (machine-to-machine), **M2P** (machine-to-person), **Digital Factory** and **Digital Supply Chain, cloud computing, Internet of Things, Big Data, robots, artificial intelligence** including **P2P** (person-to-person) and many others.

The central idea is a decentralized management model where materials, products and machines communicate with each other in real time without the need for fixed plans. Digital factories are connected online to global demand and supply chains.

The economy is completely changing its paradigm, literally every day before our eyes. New business models and **organic management systems** are increasingly reminiscent of organic natural systems, autonomous, self-diagnosing, self-adaptive, self-configuring, without unnecessary waste. It is quite clear that both the production systems and the business models as such are fundamentally changing, mainly thanks to new technologies.

Digital factory

Industry 4.0 can be perceived as a marketing concept by the German industry. However, it is not about concepts, but about customer needs. **The Digital Future Factory represents the complete digital interconnection of all levels of value-added creation - from product development to logistics.** It brings changes to the design, production and delivery of products and services to customers.

LEAN has not disappeared and will not disappear. The opposite it will finally enable a number of processes without losses and without delay, in a new form, with new approaches and tools, including Automation of ace knowledge work. There's a lot of billboards, cards, signs, lines, people, and not just that.

Listen to colleagues who lack the own ideas and thoughts, interpreting certified guidelines from literature older than 20 years, is a waste of time. **Lean Six Sigma is not sufficient enough for a long time already, instead of standardization, it is necessary to start breaking up the run-in processes.**

" The many times over used tea bag, will not make a tasty drink again."
DC VISION

Key added value

The consumer must not stand aside. Thanks to online interconnected production and logistics, the enterprise understands by using Big Data long before his needs, enables response to satisfaction or dissatisfaction in real time, immediately meet and then exceed their expectations.

Simply click on your own mobile phone, the manufacturer immediately responds to what the customer needs and which "tea" he likes best, logistics delivers fresh tea in a still hot cup.

Example of practice P.9.

In 2016 I talked to my colleague Jakub in the global SIEMENS company on innovation and on how to implement disruptive innovations. Jakub works as the Managing Director of one of the electromotor plants and complains that for 20 years he has received orders from the parent company to increase productivity by 5% per year. And such have been done so, 20 times in a row. But it is getting harder to find such improvements to their productivity. Is there still something that can be improved. Jakub did ask me when the pressure on productivity ends? Unfortunately, never, I had to answer truthfully.

Productivity growth is the driving force of the economy for thousands of years, and it will not be the same in the future. It's in the DNA of man that he wants his children to do better than their parents. And higher productivity is a tool for a better life for our children.

Permanent productivity growth is a key success factor for every manufacturing company, every business.

How to Start Automation

A number of managers are faced with the problem of how and where to begin deploying new technologies with robots and automation.

Basic levels of automation can be divided into the following 6 levels:

1. Completely manual production
2. Cells controlled by operators with automatic tools
3. Conveyor production lines
4. Partially automated conveyor lines (with workstations with operators)
5. Fully automated production lines (with operators as supervisors)
6. Highly automatic multi-function lines

Even here, it is appropriate to proceed evolutionarily. The reason is ROI (Return on Investment). It is usually problematic to estimate the ROI in big jumps ahead.

Typical areas for launching the automation process are as follows:

- Reduction of traffic (handling)
- Reducing repeated movements
- Improving quality
- Automate recurring activities

Automation of knowledge work

First of all, the first two areas concern **activities that do not add value to the customer.** And these are precisely those areas where human work is often redundant.

It is my recommendation to start eliminating new technologies by those activities that do not add value to customers.

Exercise 9 - Identification of Value Added in Process

For observing and tracking value-added activities, you can try out a practice observation form that you can download **HERE**.

Another area is the stereotypical work of office workers. It is precisely in the area of knowledge work, i.e. the work of THP staff, that a high speed of deployment of new applications, including artificial intelligence applications, can be expected.

Example of practice P.10.

At an electrical engineering firm, I asked Veronica, "What are you doing?". " I manage the logistics around the world ", I received a reply. In fact, Veronica presses an average of 4,000 times a day on the Enter button to redirect shipments. "That's why you studied college?", I suppose not. Veronica devised a software application to handle this stereotypical work, and now her work is to develop other similar applications.

8 CHAPTER

Organic Change Management Model

Agile organizations

Entrepreneurship has returned

Recently, I have seen more and more companies where management is tired at first sight. Ideas are there, everyone knows what to do. Why does it not work? Even before the implementation of any change is triggered, we learn dozens of reasons why it is not, "it is too expensive", "we do not have it." **Missing coordinated action.**

I also hear some owners complaining "Without me, the business would not prosper, only I have ideas and others just waiting for what I tell them."

If entrepreneurs are missing in the business, courses in leadership will not save it. You cannot interchange the causes and consequences. Consultations and work with managers - non - entrepreneurs are waste (MUDA).

Agile organizations use the principle of autopoieze

Management of a company of the industrial period was based on the principle of military organization. The deficiencies of this management process have been gradually weakened (decentralization, flat organizational structure, emphasis on soft management factors, etc.) but this philosophy no longer satisfies the new conditions.

Modern companies use the principle of autopoieze. The basis is the principle of **production - interconnection – distribution**, which is one of the principles of the autopoietic system. [10]

Amoeba and amoeba style management

Some organizational structures are directly designed to support innovation and face the acceleration of change at present. This is, for example, the organizational **structure of Amoeba.** [4]

Model Amoeba was applied to Kyocera. Dr. Kazuo Inamori suggested it at a time when the company began to grow, and it was necessary to divide it into smaller parts, the units called Amoebas. Leaders of Amoebas became essentially business partners.

This organizational model is based on flexibility, autonomy of internal elements, in-house and self-employment of employees. The company organizes amoebas. These are small units of 3-50 people grouped by product or job type.

Within the company, Amoebas conclude contracts with each other and compete. At the head of such companies are representatives of individual amoeba. Amoebas can freely arise and if it is found to be inefficient, it can be dissolved.

The advantage of the organizational model of amoeba is without exception huge flexibility to the external environment. At the same time, employees are led towards entrepreneurship.

It is a structure that involves all phases of the autopoietic process, the formation, association and extinction of small cells / units. [10]

AMS - Amoeba Control System

Measurement of the performance of the added value has a crucial influence on the appearance and disappearance of various amoebae. Inside the company the individual amoeba can compete with each other (i.e. Business in the company), so there is no exception that two of the amoeba can at the same time produce the same product. **Model AMS (Amoeba Management System)** using the principle of the process management is based on autonomy, agility, and self-entrepreneurship and self-management employees of [4]. Amoebas are independent units consisting of 3-50 employees operating on the three S:

- self-management,
- self-monitoring,
- self-organization.

They have a share in the profits and are applying in-house entrepreneurship. That means that an in-house market is created so that individual amoebas can compete with each other, conclude contracts and produce the same product. This system allows you to retain the advantages of a small business, such as flexibility, fast response, minimal overheads, and benefit from the big business.

What does this system remind you of? Yes, Czechs and Slovaks know the workshop of the Czechoslovak Baťa factory [11]. In his time, Bata ran his business in accordance with the principles of today's theory of autopoiesis.

Biological type enterprise

The following diagram shows the circulation of humans and amoeba in the enterprise as a living organism, in a biological type enterprise:

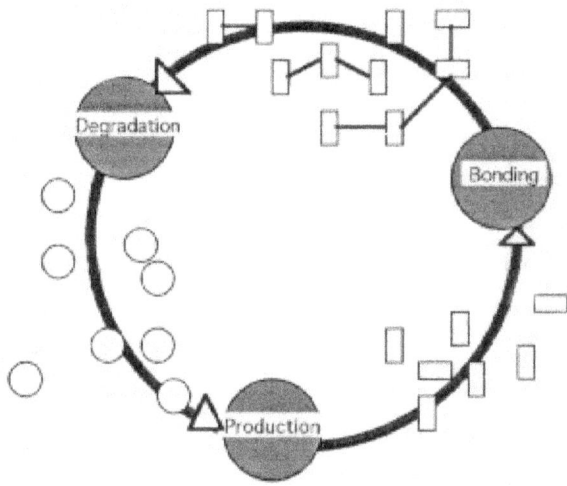

Circulation diagram of people and amoeba in the enterprise as a living organism, Source: M. Zelený

- **Enterprise Supplier** - The Enterprise Empty Container is maintained, refilled, and refurbished by controlling both input (IN) and output (OUT) processes, both from external (receiving) and internal (routing) rotation. The new members enter the stack and gradually form new amoeba or enter into the existing ones.
- **Production** - Processes of Amoeba Creation and Establishment, allocation of relevant members and resources. The Amoebas are then connected to networks, looking for supply and customer relations.
- **Bonding** - Networking and interconnection are formed: amoeba links market relationships with other amoebae, but also with customers and suppliers. An in-house market is emerging.

- **Degradation** - Processes of disconnecting, separating and extinguishing ineffective and non-functional amoebae. Some amoebas are canceled, and their members are transferred (via the stack) to the other amoeba. Others leave the business, are rotated, leased, hired, etc.

Kyocera, based in Kyótó, has become one of the world's most successful global enterprises, many times rated as the world's top not only in terms of financial performance, but also in terms of quality management and management.

The Amoeba Management System (AMS) originated in Kyocera, which had only 26 employees when it was founded in 1959. Today has tens of thousands of employees around the world and is truly a global company with sustainable profitability. Kyocera is now known as the world leader in the development and production of high-end ceramic products, from cameras to global telecommunication systems. [4]

Why does such a successful system implement only a fraction of companies in the world?

Because this system is only suitable for companies that have knowledgeable workers, as well as a number of psychological barriers play a role too.

Psychological barriers to change

As part of my practice, I have identified 4 basic barriers for the implementing of organizational changes [11]. **The first barrier** from practice is the **management 's reluctance to delegate decision-making to lower management articles.**

Many executives fear that they will not have everything under control.

Well-known Formula 1 racer Stirling Moss once said: "If you have everything under control, you probably do not go fast enough. If you want to have everything under control, you will never win races, and you may also be out of the competition. "Freedom means speed and speed means survival. At least in the new world of business that arises in today's turbulent world economy. [11]

Organically-controlled **free-form companies have** largely ceased to make a decision for the employee. An interesting fact is that, in addition to the high level of commitment and enthusiasm of employees, most of these companies show steady double-digit growth and very high loyalty to employees. [11]

Such companies include, for example, Zapos, Semco, Harley Davidson, Ideo, Google, Gore, SOL and many others, including Kyocera.

Free firm

In what differ free companies from traditional companies [11]:

MANAGEMENT SECRETS IN A TURBULENT ERA

Region	Classic firm	Free firm
Organization of the enterprise	hierarchy and not flexible sepa Leni, who perform "their" goals	above defined corporate identity and working environment in the sense of corporate identity decentralization standards, work in autonomous teams or in networks
Workers	employees who receive tasks and goals for their satisfies her get reward	co-entrepreneurs who define the tasks and goals themselves, and hence the amount of their reward
Leaders	strong leaders who set the direction and goals, monitor their fulfillment	humble leaders who create conditions for people to develop their talent at work
Motivation to achieve common goals	stimulating money to achieve goals	Search through motivation towards meeting the sense of the common vision
Work discipline	standards, working rules, control	responsibility and respect for colleagues and customers, self-discipline
Troubleshooting and Conflicts	compromise = I, or you = I (50%) + ty (50%) = 50% formal meetings and infor mation system, discussions in which it is usually right boss	synergies (third alternative) = I and you = I (100%) + ty (100%) = 200% free information sharing Napa DU informal communication, dialogue, different perspectives
Education	Plans staff development, training, evaluation great peers, education is often focused on information, not knowledge	p racing player defines his / her own development and looks for a suitable position, 360 degree feedback from lessons from the past
Management and control	superiority / subordination, distrust, top-down control, control of people and results	f ere, respect, mutual respect, focus on common results, moral and ethical principles
Working environment	with a high-defined corporate identity and work environment in the sense of corporate identity standards	of the employees create a working environment in which they feel good - such as home-like devices. a reading room, a circle, a meditation room,
Work and its content	p ORK position descriptions and working standards, working time defined	about the workload defined by the employee himself and also looking for a suitable job in the company, the working time does not exist, if the work allows, it can work from home

Psychological barriers to change

Further barriers are both staffing and management [11]. In addition to the general reluctance to leave the comfort zone, the most common obstacle to successful change is fear, which takes on a variety of forms.

A common barrier to change is the **fear of having a vision**. A vision is a dream, a destination that a worker can set. Many workers, however, are afraid and prefer to stay in the crowd, in their safe reality without any change. These people need to be encouraged to change in their search for their vision.

The third barrier is **fear of failure**. Some people have vision sets in the organic system, then often the vision to be successful in finding suitable tasks and positions, but then prefer to remain passive, but to set out to the realization of his vision. If only remain passive, they are not get exposed to the risk, that the community will refuse them, for example. *" you do not have this the job or position "*.

The fourth barrier is **fear of the reaction of the environment**. What will the others say about the change? Will I manage to "hunt" enough of the projects on the internal market, I have a firm position in my amoeba, but how will the neighborhood look at it, my colleagues?

To develop a positive change, you need to have a feeling of dissatisfaction with the current state, the ability to overcome your fear of change, and take a proverbial first step. [11]

Cultural aspects of change

Example from practice P.11.

In 2013, I decided to apply the principles of amoeba management directly in my own consulting company. Very early I recognized my own psychological barriers and resistance in my own company. Many employees protested strongly, many of them immediately left the company. The most common argument against change was the element of internal competition. Employees argued that they wanted to cooperate, not to compete, there was a huge unacknowledged concern about whether everyone as a businessman would be able to help himself.

In spite of considerable resistance, I have enforced the new model, based on teams, not individuals. The firm diminished radically in size, but found its new equilibrium and without unnecessary conflicts, it was much more profitable than ever before.

Depending on those cultural practices it is possible to find more **individual agility in the Anglo-Saxon world**, which is traditionally strongly individualistic. **In a European or Asian environment, it is appropriate to form teams and help with change through teamwork.** [11]

Agile managing system

For effective implementation, we need to consider whether this system is suitable for the company. If the company is in a combined environment, then it is definitely not recommendable.

There is no management theory to implement the autopoietic management system. Managers of **Kyocera, Jakob Schlapfer & Co AG** or Czech **GiTy** simply responded to the market situation, trying to implement an agile management system using the trial & error method. [9]

Nevertheless, **three basic elements of the organic management system** can be traced:

- Measuring value added at cell level
- a flat organizational structure with the 3S principle
- the existence of managerial rules and discipline and their observance

A typical representative of such a company is Apple. Steve Jobs has dubbed Apple as the world's largest Start-Up, with 30,000 employees. **Every employee of Apple is an entrepreneur who at the time works only on one task or project.**

And this is an absolute focus on one important thing, it's about setting priorities.

The Organic Change Management Model

Switching to a business as a living entity is not easy, it is not enough to upload new software to your computer. The author of the change management model in this section is prof. Milan Zelený [11], which has long been reviving Baťa's business principles.

Nature does not change everything, it changes what it does not need. Therefore, the company should start changing what is not the key, what is not needed, or what does not bring the expected results, in which the expended efforts are outweighed at the end of the project with few or no benefits.

1. **It is necessary to maintain what is necessary for the functioning of the company (core of the company - knowledge / skills and values) and to immediately reduce those parts that are affected by the state of " inertia ".**

How to define the kernel? Just remember the question in what we are best in the world, what we do well and what links us in the company, which values.

Once the essential areas that must be preserved are known, then the change can be handled efficiently. **We cannot know what to change if we do not know what to preserve.**

2. **For the new structure to work, it is necessary to create clear rules for the behavior of managers and employees, to create clear guidelines for decision-making competencies.**

The new agile organizational structure can often lead to the feeling that now nobody instructs managers and that they can do anything they think best. It's not like that, **moderation applies.**

3. **Introduce the principle of improvement**

The set rules of authority and line of authority are not forever. In a cyclical economy, market behavior needs to be adapted to the needs of customers. Get Kaizen, improvement is a matter for all employees.

4. **Create a system for monitoring the internal and external market**

A living organism is able to receive signals from within and from outside in multiple ways, with more parts of its organism. It is similar in the company. It is necessary to set up a system that listens to the internal customer (employees) as well as external customers. Above these signals it is necessary to make regular meetings, make decisions, which signals need to be addressed and go into coordinated action.

These four principles form the core of a business.

5. **Establish a system of training and education for existing and new employees**

It is much easier to build a new firm on the new rules than to reconstruct the existing one. It is therefore necessary to start training existing employees on new rules and restrictions, as well as to change the recruitment process and the initial training of new employees. As in the LEAN environment, I have always recommended that you are required to engage in continuous improvement in employment contracts, so it is appropriate to incorporate the rules of conduct and values into employment contracts. Like Bat'a, who had an obligation to work in and out of work contracts.

6. **Learning organizations**

Explain and consistently reinforce the importance of basic standards, forms, systems and structures of management, communication and experience. The business is now ready to learn and educate.

7. **Motivation system**

Introduce incentives and rewards for the excellent implementation and performance of individuals and groups while respecting the core values of the kernel and adapting them to new structures.

Example from practice P.12.

In 2015, I worked as a transformation manager of an international engineering group based in Malmö. The owner of the corporation was a venture capital fund, which usually implies a tremendous pressure on the creation of profits. The company was faltering around red zero, not only the owners, but the banks were also very nervous. I have proposed the introduction of a very simple motivation system for all employees, based on a share in increasing labor productivity. **In terms of market, it was necessary to increase productivity by at least 10%.** The motivation principle was simple, **30% of the financial benefit of increasing productivity for the company will be the share paid to employees.** Productivity in manufacturing was measured by the portion of norm hours sold and consumed norm-hours (Sold / Spent). It was important to persuade laborers to stop saving hours, but to start shortening them.

Productivity started to increase immediately, just 2 months after the introduction of the new system, it was up 12%. We subsequently improved the system and introduced other indicators, such as improving quality and reducing Lead time and other Just-in-Time concepts.

8. **Recognize and reward exceptional people for extraordinary services and leadership**, whether socially, publicly or privately, to re-establish a sustainable organizational culture. [11]

This is quite complicated in Central and Eastern European conditions. The principle of "rather not been seen" is still strongly rooted in people.

Here, it is appropriate to recall the **basic 3 principles of motivation:**

- **Being heard** - a capable manager listens to his people

- **To be understood** - it is not enough to just listen, it is necessary to have empathy and to understand people, to understand their needs and to try to help them
- **Be recognized** - in European conditions, it is very often enough to thank for a well-done job, ideally in front of other team members or individually.

9. **Start building the principles of a free business**, freeing out external forms of enforcement and coercion, providing more freedom, and gradually allowing self-discipline, cooperative pressure, and a sense of corporate belonging and identity to replace external authority.

Free business does not mean in any case that everyone does what they want, it's not about putting your feet on the table and lighting the candle.

10. **Recognize and support each individual in the direction of personal and corporate growth and internal fulfillment within the enterprise.** Individuals' ownership of an enterprise is an expression of work / life balance. [11]

We need to follow new trends in the young generation Y. This generation has new demands for work and only really agile companies will be able to meet them. It is not just about the requirement of home office, flexible working hours, or leisure time, sports and environmental concerns, generation Y brings almost a revolution to the perception of work and the working environment.

Example of practice P.13.

During my visit to our branch office in Lyon, France, I was confronted with completely new trends in employee benefits. Employees did not ask for a passenger car for personal purposes, because **driving a car is no longer in**. Everybody rides on bicycles and therefore they want cycling infrastructure, they want only organic meals in the canteen, they want to have space to work in the garden or simply stay and live in the canteen. Nobody wanted their own desk to work on, with drawers and file cabinets, because all the documents are in his tablet. It is a requirement, to have a sabbatical leave of at least 6 months, so that employees can reap the energy and ideas for further work. This is not a dream of the future, it is the reality of the present.

One piece flow

The company Toyota came to realize more than 50 years ago that is much more efficient to produce in small batches " **one piece flow** " (one-piece flow) than in mass production (mass production). [5]

This is well described in the book "How Toyota Does It" by Jeffey Liker [5] on the example of children and fathers who stick the envelopes with invitations to family get together. While the children want to first put all the invitations in the envelopes and then seal all the envelopes at once, the father will propose a competition and he will complete and stick the envelopes one by one. In this small race for a time the father will win. **You can start up dozens of new projects or tasks, but few can do it quickly to the end.** Incomplete tasks are the same as surplus stocks and therefore waste (MUDA).

"Every employee works at one time on one project only" Steve Jobs, Apple

Priorities and Kanban

At first, try changing the way you set priorities. Inspire in Kanban [5] and establish a **new system based on real managerial capacity**. How many tasks are you able to accomplish in real time? Try to solve projects and tasks gradually and never exceed your capacity. [7]

Task Tray	Tasks in solution (Do)	Checked	Verified (Improve)
D E F	B C	AND	

The maximum managerial capacity set is 3 tasks / projects / product benefits, etc. It is not possible to start more than 3 projects at a time. Only after completion of Task A, another task can be put into resolution to complement the capacity to solve 3 tasks.

Task Tray	Tasks in solution (Do)	Checked	Verified (Improve)
F G H	C D E	B	AND

At the end, you will find that the whole process of upgrading a new product, a new process, or simply fulfilling a business strategy will go a long way. [7]

To reach the ultimate success, the need for more is definitely there. For example, to introduce customer driven measurements and a whole series of other cognitive strategies.

Exercise 10 - Kanban for task management

Try the PDCA kanban action plan according to the task Tray.

9 CHAPTER

Summary and recommendations of the coordinated action

Managerial summary

The whole text is constantly returning to a turbulent environment, to a constantly changing market, to a cyclical movement on the principles of autopoieze that will never end. The summary is a list of basic principles that should be remembered from time to time and to avoid unnecessary fears of chaos, because even **in chaos can be found order and learn to predict and manage.**

For over 20 years, I have implemented Lean philosophy and Lean Six Sigma tools. The world has changed very quickly, and the effectiveness of the Lean tools has been getting smaller and smaller. Nevertheless, Lean's tools are still effective. Their history dates back several centuries to the Buddhist temples, where Buddhist monks and story tellers - the **Kamishibai** were travelling from the city to city to tell their stories through the help of cards.

In the corporate environment, Kamishibai is used as a board for placing T-shaped cards. They are used to quickly preview the status of important production parameters or services. These parameters can be set for different areas of trim control.

This is a very effective method, so I am presenting this managerial summary in the form of 10 cards, which together form a set of important parameters for building a corporate management system.

Benefits cards are in that company management will get an overview of the sites on key parameters such as the security, maintenance status, productivity, quality, cost and try to help solve the problems of the employees. Employees know what the workplace requires and unite in the approach to work.

Managerial summary

Kamishibai Key Cards for Building an Organic Business Management System:

#1 Organic Thinking (Think Organic)
Essential change in management thinking from "mechanical" to "organic". The company is a living organism, not a machine. A successful enterprise is more a part of biology and evolution than industrial engineering. Not LEAN, but agile corporate culture leads to long-term prosperity.

#2 Knowledge is coordinated action
Knowledge is not a description of the action (cookbook), but it is a coordinated action (the ability to cook). Knowledge management = knowing why, knowing how and what + actions, not process schemes, are the result of change. The prosperity base is to have knowledgeable staff capable of action.

#3 The principle of autopoiesis
It is necessary to establish rules for the creation, connection for actions and cell death, to define cells as individuals or teams, to establish rules for the reduction or "death" of the cell if it does not bring added value and results. Even the human cell has the term of its death (apoptosis).

#4 Agile corporate culture
Set behavior rules for internal network cell functioning, implement and maintain LEAN philosophy and cell-level tools on a daily basis. It is also necessary to define the corporate values on which the firm is built and which will be followed consistently.

Managerial summary

Kamishibai Key Cards for Building an Organic Business Management System:

#5 Strategy and attributes of modulation
Create a map of key activities (Porter's Key Activity Map). Build a "point of difference" - differentiate yourself from competitors (activity map, compliance and differentiation attributes, benchmarking), develop differentiation attributes, and keep track of customer and competitor.

#6 The principle of collocation
The company is part of a global network of suppliers and customers. It is necessary to have rules for the operation of vendor integration (SCM) in its own supply chain, adapting to the worldwide tendency of supplier collocation (single-chain integration).

#7 Own product with added value
If an enterprise does not have its own product or service, it does not have a brand and has no access to the customer, then it is "fitting" from its definition. Only R & D can enable us to elevate from this position. The activities with the lowest added value are production and assembly, R & D and customer service have the highest added value.

#8 Innovation without implementation is hallucination
Innovations that do not increase competitiveness or add value and increase productivity are not innovations. Innovations without implementation are not innovation, just ideas in the drawer.

Managerial summary

Kamishibai Key Cards for Building an Organic Business Management System:

#9 Kanban for task management
At first, try changing the way you set priorities. Inspire in Kanban and set up a new system based on real managerial capacity. Try to solve projects and tasks gradually and never exceed your capacity.

#10 Accelerating the emergence of new technologies
Everything that can be digital will become digital, and it will happen soon. Artificial intelligence systems will replace not only stereotypical work but also knowledgeable workers. Accelerating the take-off of new technologies into production, transport, logistics, healthcare and other industries can no longer be stopped. Artificial intelligence will achieve higher performance than people already by 2030 (Ray Kurzweil, The singularity is near).

Where KamishiBai T cards have two sides - the green side indicates the status OK, the principle in the company is currently working. If this is not the case, the card is placed on the notice board with the red side facing the front.

Exercise 11 - KamishiBai

It is now possible to test the T cards and perform a small audit on their own company. Create 10 cards, green on one side and red on the other side. After that, the manager can evaluate himself how the business is, how many cards he attaches to the board with a red color in advance, and how many will be after the evaluation of the greens. For evaluation, you need to ask yourself " **What is the potential for improvement in this area?** ". If the potential is relatively small, then glows green card ☐

Managerial summary

For the long-term prosperity of the business, it is necessary to work in all areas at the same time. Business agility status cannot be evaluated by just the number of green or red cards, they can only direct and identify certain priorities at a given moment.

These were the basic principles and trends I have observed in successful companies in turbulent environments. If a firm is in a continuous environment, it can be managed mechanically, but in chaos or fluid modernity the mechanical principle of control is unsustainable for a long time.

This is the basic paradox. In the chaos managers have a tendency to get everything under control, and it often according to the rules, what I will not do myself, I do not. These attitudes may not be enough in the long run, and companies such as Kyocera, Apple, or Google have shown that mechanical approaches may not be the most effective.

LEAN itself is long enough. On contrary, the dogmatic concept of leading Lean Six Sigma companies into ever deeper states of their own, from which it is still difficult to change the company.

Linear thinking is FINALLY superseded by thinking cyclic. It is necessary to know not only why this is happening but also how to use it.

The wind rises, hold onto your hats! :o)

"Some are building windbreakers, against the winds, we look forward to the ever-stronger winds and tension the bigger sails"
Jens Vasehus, Implement Consulting Group

Finally

Dear readers,

Thank you for reading the Paperback book.

I hope it has brought you new knowledge, benefits and inspiration for your managerial decision-making.

If you are interested autopoiesis principle and want to know more, follow the articles on my blog, where you can find more information and examples from practice.

If you do not like something about this book and you tell us, we'll be grateful. Simply write your opinion to impactive@protonmail.com.

You will really please us even more if you tell us and others that you liked the book, for example by reviewing the book on Amazon.

Thank you.

Libor Witassek

© Libor Witassek, 2018

Recommended literature

In my observations, I used the following publications:

1) BROŽ, D. (2011). Transformace firemní kultury, Praha, Moderní řízení 2011/6: 22-25.

2) BAUMAN,Z.: Tekutá modernita. Mladá Fronta, Praha 2002.

3) DRUCKER,P.F.: Řízení v turbulentní době. Management Press 1994

4) ISHIDA, H. „Amoeba Management at KYOCERA Corporation", Human Systems Management, 1994.

5) LIKER, Jeffrey K. The Toyota way : 14 management principles from the world. New York : McGraw-Hill , 2007. 330 s. ISBN 0-07-139231-9.

6) PETERS,T.J.: Thriving on Chaos – Handbook for a Management Revolution. Macmillan, New York 1987

7) RIESE, E., The Lean Start-Up

8) TRUNEČEK,J.: Znalostní podnik ve znalostní společnosti. Professional publishing, Praha 2003

9) TRUNEČEK, J. 2008. Možnosti transferu vybraných vědeckých teorií do managementu, Ekonomika a management 2008/3

10) ZELENÝ,M.: Autopoiesis (sebeorganizace) v sítích malých a středních podniků. www.darius.cz/ag_nikola/beseda40.html

11) ZELENÝ, Milan a Ján KOŠTURIAK. *To vám byl divný svět...*. Praha: NLN, s.r.o., 2012. ISBN 978-80-7422-171-2.

List of abbreviations

Benchmarking is an expression for comparing business performance.

The CEO (Chief Executive Officer) is the top manager in the company

Just-in-time is a system for achieving the best possible quality, cost and delivery of products and services by eliminating all forms of mud within in-house processes and delivering products just in time according to customer requirements (internal and external).

Kaizen is a Japanese term meaning "change for the better". Applied to business organizations, it means constant improvement involving anyone who does not have the power, possibly no money.

Kamishibai is used as a blackboard for the T- shaped card, they can be used to quickly preview the status of important production parameters or services. These parameters can be set for different areas of trim control.

Kanban is a communications tool in "just in time" production and the inventory control system developed by Taiichi Ohn at Toyota. Kanban, a "label", is linked to a specific part of the production line where it indicates the supply of a certain quantity.

MUDA is a Japanese expression for waste, for unnecessary losses.

SCM means **Supply Chain Management** - Global **Supply Chain Management**

ABOUT THE AUTHOR

Libor Witassek has long been specializing in the area of second order cybernetics with a focus on managing the business as a living organism. He worked as an advisor to the American Wharton University of Pennsylvania for a business program in Central Europe.

Libor Witassek also served as Chairman of Managing Partners, the leading consultancy group Allied Consultants Europe e.V. Libor is an expert in building business management systems. Lean Six Sigma has helped several dozen global companies, such as Siemens, Foxconn, Velux, or Johnson & Controls. He worked as a transformation manager at the global corporation GCE Group and CEO in the machinery business VÍTKOVICE MACHINERY GROUP.

Libor Witassek is the author of several publications and LEAN Leadership® methodology, which he lectures at the University of Economics in Prague. Libor holds a number of awards including, among others, the Czech Republic's competition of Manager of the year 2012, Marketer of the Year 2011 and 2012 and a Corporate Social Responsibility Award in the Moravian-Silesian Region 2013.

Today, Libor Witassek is an independent entrepreneur within the IMPACTIVE® investment company.

www.ingramcontent.com/pod-product-compliance
Lightning Source LLC
Chambersburg PA
CBHW070402230526
45471CB00006B/2662